Hello, Friend!

Disclaimer:
This book is a work of fiction. Characters, names, places, and
events are products of the author's imagination. Any
resemblance to real persons, living or dead, is purely coincidental
—unless the person in question told me a really funny joke that
had to make it into this book.

For everyone gathered 'round my table—
especially Truman, Scott, and the one
who never stops asking for treats, Piper!

Eat, drink, and be weird!

How to use this book!

Sometimes after a long day, the grown-ups at your table might feel tired, and your brain might be full of mashed potatoes or school stuff—making dinner talk feel tricky! One time when I was a kid, I forgot to tell my Mom about how milk came out of Josh's nose at lunch and Jessica almost puked because of it! Hahaha!

This book is here to help everyone share fun ideas and big laughs. Inside, you'll discover 365 wacky, wonderful questions. Some will make you think super deeply, and others will have you giggling out loud—so every night at the table becomes a brand-new adventure!

Two Easy Ways to Play!

1. Go in Order
   Flip to the next page each night and discover a brand-new question to discuss.

2. Pick at Random
   Can't decide? Close your eyes, open the book, and let your finger choose the question. You can fill in the numbered bubble on the checklist page, so you can track which questions you've done!

Rules

1. There really aren't any rules.
2. Each night, pick a designated question-picker and a question-reader. This can be the same person, or different people. Maybe each one gets to wear a wizard hat!
3. Encourage everyone to share-big siblings, little siblings, grown-ups, and guests!
4. There are no wrong answers: let your imagination run wild!
5. Laugh together, think together, and learn something new about each other.
6. Keep this book by your plate and let it guide your conversations-one question at a time.
7. If you want to doodle, draw, or write your answers in this book, go ahead (won't it be fun to look at this when you're 30!).
8. Remember to try new foods, dream big, and stay wonderfully weird!

Question Checklist

(1) (2) (3) (4) (5) (6) (7) (8) (9) (10)
(11) (12) (13) (14) (15) (16) (17) (18) (19) (20)
(21) (22) (23) (24) (25) (26) (27) (28) (29) (30)
(31) (32) (33) (34) (35) (36) (37) (38) (39) (40)
(41) (42) (43) (44) (45) (46) (47) (48) (49) (50)
(51) (52) (53) (54) (55) (56) (57) (58) (59) (60)
(61) (62) (63) (64) (65) (66) (67) (68) (69) (70)
(71) (72) (73) (74) (75) (76) (77) (78) (79) (80)
(81) (82) (83) (84) (85) (86) (87) (88) (89) (90)
(91) (92) (93) (94) (95) (96) (97) (98) (99) (100)
(101) (102) (103) (104) (105) (106) (107) (108) (109) (110)
(111) (112) (113) (114) (115) (116) (117) (118) (119) (120)
(121) (122) (123) (124) (125) (126) (127) (128) (129) (130)
(131) (132) (133) (134) (135) (136) (137) (138) (139) (140)
(141) (142) (143) (144) (145) (146) (147) (148) (149) (150)
(151) (152) (153) (154) (155) (156) (157) (158) (159) (160)
(161) (162) (163) (164) (165) (166) (167) (168) (169) (170)
(171) (172) (173) (174) (175) (176) (177) (178) (179) (180)
(181) (182)

Question Checklist

(183) (184) (185) (186) (187) (188) (189) (190) (191) (192)
(193) (194) (195) (196) (197) (198) (199) (200) (201) (202)
(203) (204) (205) (206) (207) (208) (209) (210) (211) (212)
(213) (214) (215) (216) (217) (218) (219) (220) (221) (222)
(223) (224) (225) (226) (227) (228) (229) (230) (231) (232)
(233) (234) (235) (236) (237) (238) (239) (240) (241) (242)
(243) (244) (245) (246) (247) (248) (249) (250) (251) (252)
(253) (254) (255) (256) (257) (258) (259) (260) (261) (262)
(263) (264) (265) (266) (267) (268) (269) (270) (271) (272)
(273) (274) (275) (276) (277) (278) (279) (280) (281) (282)
(283) (284) (285) (286) (287) (288) (289) (290) (291) (292)
(293) (294) (295) (296) (297) (298) (299) (300) (301) (302)
(303) (304) (305) (306) (307) (308) (309) (310) (311) (312)
(313) (314) (315) (316) (317) (318) (319) (320) (321) (322)
(323) (324) (325) (326) (327) (328) (329) (330) (331) (332)
(333) (334) (335) (336) (337) (338) (339) (340) (341) (342)
(343) (344) (345) (346) (347) (348) (349) (350) (351) (352)
(353) (354) (355) (356) (357) (358) (359) (360) (361) (362)
(363) (364) (365)

Question #1

What would the world be like if everyone was kind every day?

Question #2

What would your superhero name be?

Question #3

What's
your
favorite
thing
about
winter?

Question #4

If you invented a
new emoji,
what would it
look like?

Question #5

What's something
about this dinner

that makes you
feel thankful
right now?

Question #6

What kind of animal would be the worst dinner guest-and why?

Question #7

If you could visit your future self in high school, what would you want to know?

Question #8

If you could only eat one food for a whole week, what would you choose?

Question #9

If you could
be famous
for something,
what would
it be?

Question #10

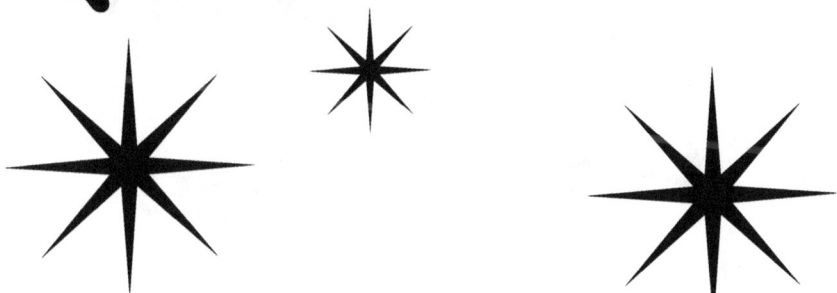

What makes you feel most loved during the holidays?

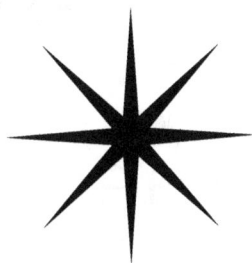

Question #11

Pancakes

OR

Waffles?

Question #12

What's something new you've learned about a friend at school?

Question #13

What's your favorite thing about fall?

Question #14

If you could ask the smartest person one question, what would it be?

Question #15

If you could paint your room any color, what would it be?

Question #16

If you had a fairy godparent, what would you wish for?

Question #17

If you could plant a garden that grows anything, what would it grow?

Question #18

What's the best high-five moment you had this week?

Question #19

You wake up as a giant-what's the first thing you do?

Question #20

What's the silliest job you can imagine?

Question #21

What if every kid had to choose a royal title like "Duke of Donuts"?

Question #22

☀ ☀ ☀ ☀ ☀

What's the very first thing you want to do on the first day of summer?

Question #23

If you could visit any place in the world, where would you go first?

Question #24

Would you rather sneeze glitter or burp bubbles?

Question #25

What's your favorite part of dinnertime?

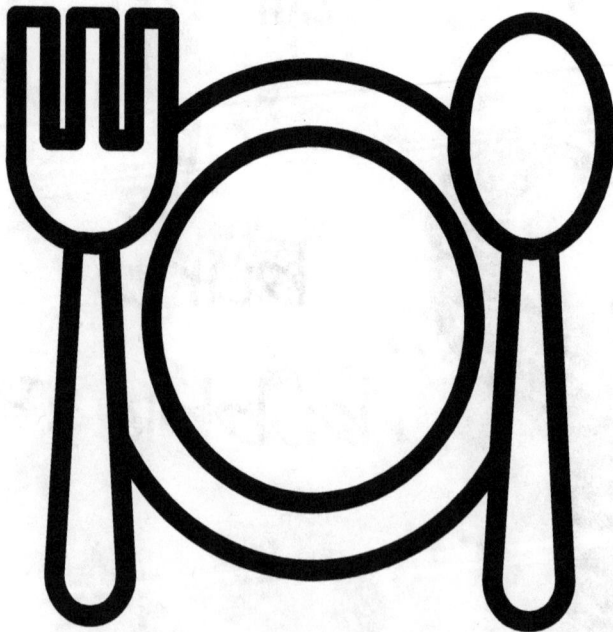

Draw Dinner Tonight!

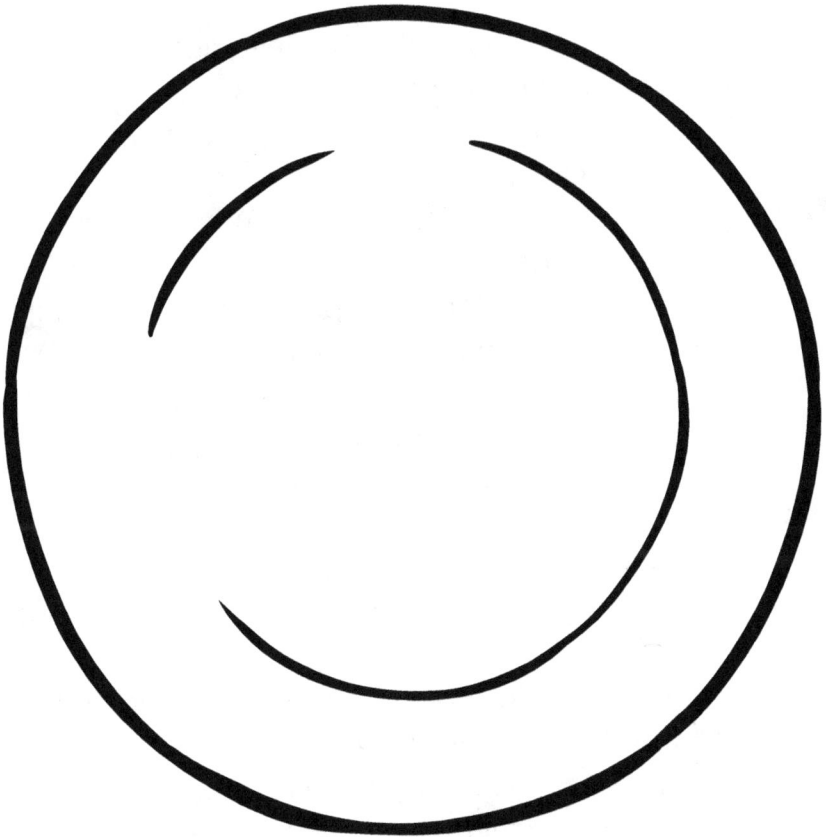

Did you know?

Impress people with this cool info!

- Watermelons can float in water because they're about 25% air!
- Peanuts aren't true nuts at all but legumes—more closely related to beans than almonds.
- Broccoli is actually the flower of its plant, right before the blooms open.
- When you crunch on celery, you're munching on its stem—nature's crispy straw!
- The durian fruit is so famously pungent it's banned in many hotels and public transit systems.
- Pineapple contains the enzyme bromelain, which can tenderize meat (and make your tongue tingle).
- The summer squash we call zucchini in the U.S. is known as courgette in the U.K.
- Bananas are true berries botanically, while strawberries aren't—even though they wear their seeds outside!
- Cook red cabbage in very alkaline water and it'll turn bright blue—food science magic!
- Vermicelli means "little worms" in Italian, though it tastes nothing like them!

Question #26

What does being kind mean to you?

Question #27

What would your superhero costume look like?

Question #28

If you could build the world's coolest snowman, what would it look like?

Question #29

Create an invention to help people who are afraid of the dark.

Question #30

What was something that made you smile today?

Question #31

What would a snake do for fun if it had arms?

Question #32

If a time traveler came to dinner, what would you feed them?

Question #33

What's the weirdest food you've ever tried-or want to try?

Question #34

DREAM

What's one word that describes your biggest dream?

Question #35

Would you rather wear glittery clothes for a week or sing carols every time you talk?

Question #36

Ice cream cone

or

Ice cream sandwich?

Question #37

Did anything unexpected happen at school today?

Question #38

If you could jump into a giant pile of anything, what would it be?

Question #39

What's more important: kindness or honesty?

Question #40

What's your favorite thing to do on a rainy day at home?

Question #41

What magical creature would be your best friend?

Question #42

What's the first thing you notice when spring begins?

Question #43

What's something you used to avoid, but now you face head-on?

Question #44

You have a magic marker—whatever you draw becomes real. What do you draw first?

Question #45

Would you rather be a baker, a builder, or a balloon artist?

Question #46

If school could only be taught by animals, which one should be the math teacher?

Question #47

What does summer taste like?

Question #48

Who is someone you'd love to spend a day with?

Question #49

Would you rather find a treasure chest or a magic wand?

Question #50

What's one thing you think makes your dinnertime unique?

The Tale of the Forbidden Page...

Deep within the dusty covers of "A Question A Day: Dinnertime Edition," a rumor whispers of page 405. No child who opens this book may ever glance its inked secrets. At night, candlelight flickers on words that shift and shimmer, refusing discovery. Legends say a single syllable on that page can summon giggling shadows and upside-down spoons dancing across the table. Parents hush siblings who inch toward that corner; librarians stiffen with fear. The story warns: curiosity invites a chorus of ravenous crumbs and cheeky ants. So clamp the book shut, ignore its thumping in the shelf. Never, ever read page 405!

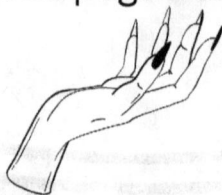

BINGO!

B	I	N	G	O
Knife	Seconds	Stove	Please.	Plate
Story	Dessert	Cleanup	Napkin	Candle
Side Dish	Tradition	Free Space	Sauce	Pass the...
Thank you!	Spoon	Pot/Pan	Fridge	Cup
Seasoning	Recipe	Tupperware	Fork	Leftovers

Dinner Bingo: How to Play

Place the card in the center and grab markers—stickers, tokens, or even little dabs of sauce. As you chat, listen for words on the card (fork, seconds, please) and dab them off. Work together to complete a straight line—horizontal, vertical, or diagonal—or race to fill every square before dessert. You can also play solo and time yourself to see how fast you can bingo! Celebrate with cheers, extra corn, or ice cream.

Ready, set, dab!

Question #51

When was the last time someone did something kind for you?

Question #52

If you had a superpower only during dinner, what would it be?

Question #53

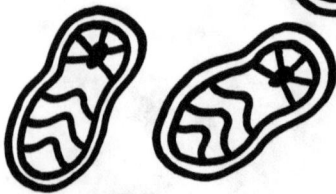
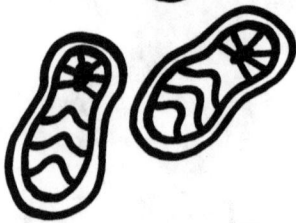

Would
you rather
have a
snowball fight
or go
sledding?

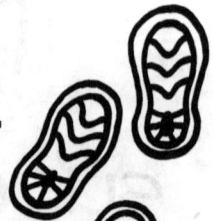
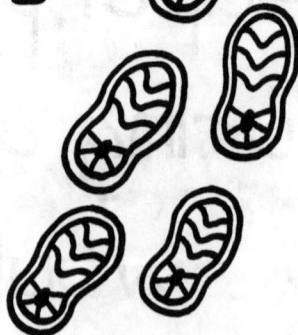

Question #54

Invent a flavor of gum that does something cool when you chew it.

Question #55

Who is someone you're thankful for and why?

Question #56

What would a goat do if it became a YouTube star?

Question #57

If you went back to the first Thanksgiving, what would you bring to share?

Question #58

If you invented a brand-new ice cream flavor, what would it be?

Question #59

If you could start your own company, what would it be?

Question #60

What's your favorite way to count down to a holiday?

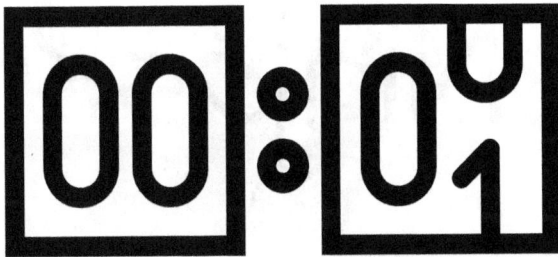

00:01

Question #61

Pirates

OR

Ninjas?

Question #62

What subject makes you feel super smart?

Question #63

What color do you think fall smells like?

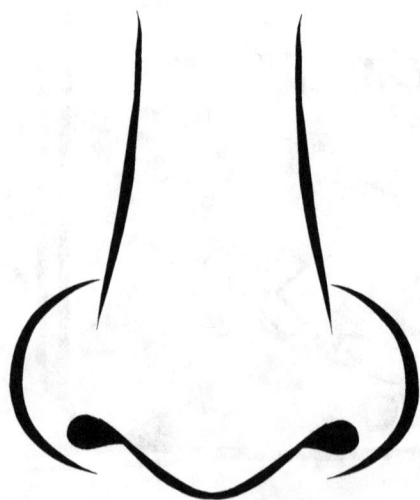

Question #64

What makes something "true"?

Question #65

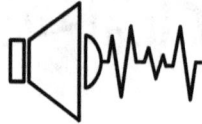

If your fridge had a voice, what would it say when you open it?

Question #66

If you were a wizard, what spell would you cast first?

Question #67

What's your favorite thing about spring weather?

Question #68

What's your best score or time in any game, activity, or test?

A+

Question #69

What would your royal title be if you ruled a kingdom?

Question #70

If animals had jobs,
what would your
pet be great at?

Question #71

What if every time someone said "hello," they had to spin in a circle?

Question #72

Would you rather eat popsicles every day or swim every day?

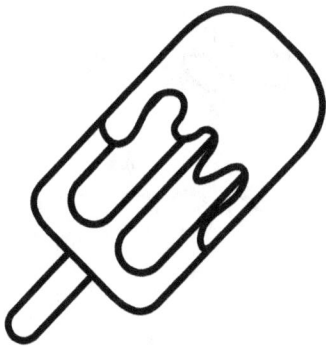

Question #73

What's the friendliest place you've ever been?

Question #74

Would you rather eat only one color of food or never eat your favorite food again?

? ? ?

Question #75

What kind of restaurant would your family open together?

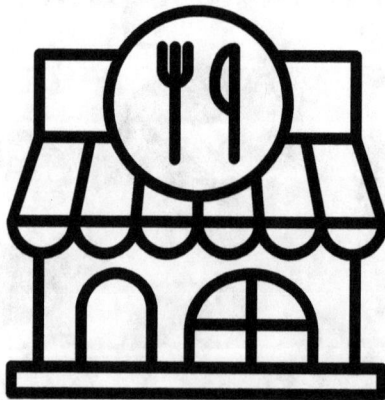

Yuk it Up!

Why did the tomato turn red?

Because it saw the salad dressing!

What's a pirate's favorite side dish?

Arrrr-tichokes!

Why did the cereal break up with the milk?

It found someone butter!

What did the noodle say to the tomato?

"Pasta la vista, baby!"

What's a ghost's favorite dinner?

Spook-ghetti!

How do you organize a space dinner?

You planet!

What did the grape say when it got stepped on?

Nothing-it just let out a little wine!

Question #76

How do you feel when you're kind to someone?

Question #77

If you could freeze time, what would you do while everything else was paused?

Question #78

What's your ultimate snow day snack?

Snack Time

Question #79

Make up a gadget that could help clean your room instantly.

Question #80

What's a simple thing you're glad you have?

Question #81

What would a hamster pack for vacation?

Question #82

Would you rather visit the Ice Age or the far future?

Question #83

What's your dream birthday dinner?

Question #84

What would your dream house look like?

Question #85

What's the most fun you've ever had during a holiday?

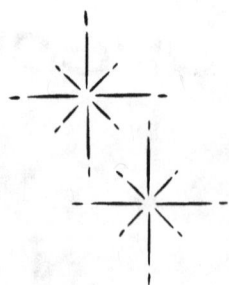

Question #86

Cats

or

Dogs?

Question #87

What's one thing you learned today that surprised you?

Question #88

What's your dream Halloween costume?

Question #89

Can you think of a problem that doesn't have a solution yet?

?

Question #90

If you could switch rooms with someone for a day, who would it be?

Question #91

What kind of
magic potion would
you invent?

Question #92

Would you rather splash in puddles or roll in the grass?

Question #93

What's something you cooked, baked, or helped make that turned out super good?

Question #94

You find a treasure map under your plate- where does it lead?

Question #95

What job do you think is the most fun in the world?

Question #96

What if there was a rule that you had to high-five everyone you saw...even squirrels?

Question #97

What's your dream summer vacation?

Question #98

If you could visit outer space or the bottom of the ocean, which would you choose?

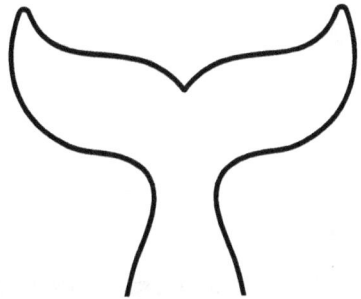

Question #99

Would you rather be able to pause time or rewind it?

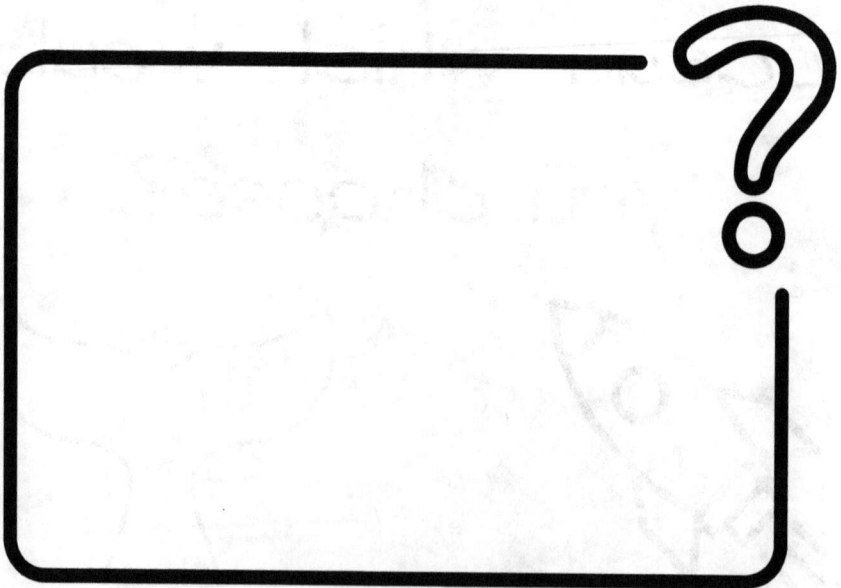

Question #100

If you had to rate tonight's meal with stars, how many would it get?

☆☆☆☆☆

Draw Your Family!

Grab your pencils and sketch each family member with their funniest quirks—big grins, wild hair, even your pet's waggy tail or draw yourself as a friendly alien: three eyes, sparkly tentacles for hair, and glowing antennae waving hello!

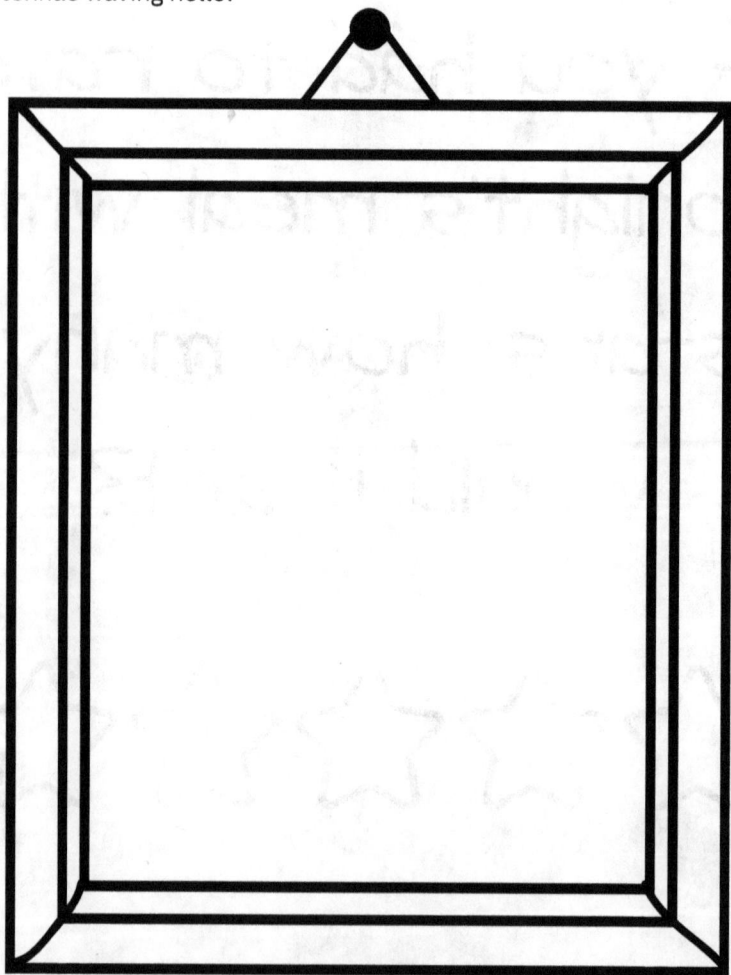

Use these 3 panels to tell any story you like! Maybe draw your little sister telling the world her silliest joke—like insisting that socks are ticklish—or show your hamster zooming down the hallway on tiny roller skates, squeaking for speed. You're the author, artist, and director of your very own comic adventure!

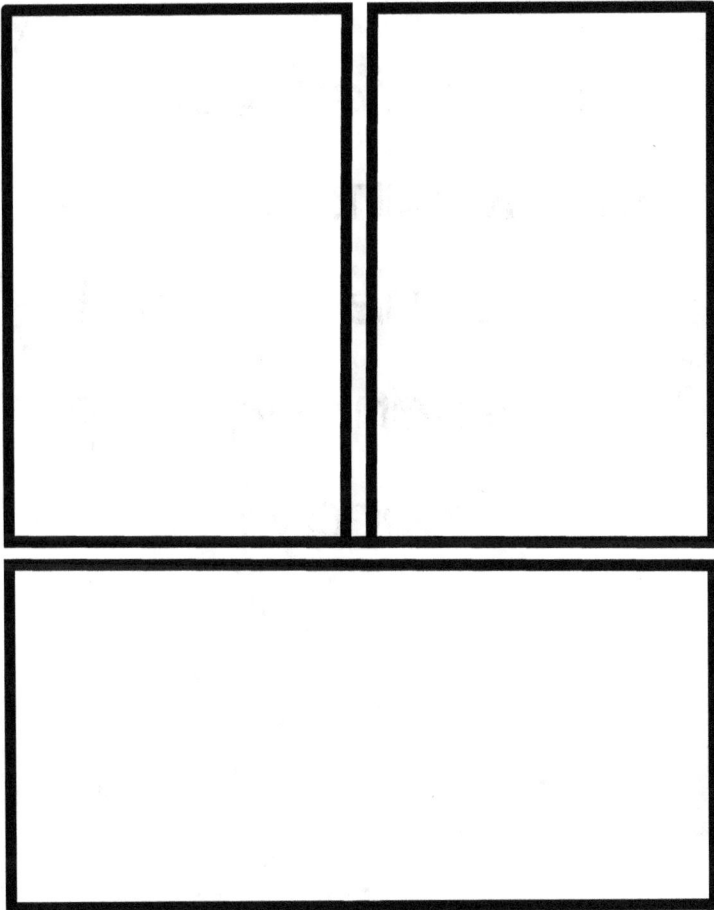

Question #101

How can you show kindness to someone without spending money?

Question #102

If you could shapeshift into anything, what would you pick first?

Question #103

SNOW

If snow were a different color, what color should it be?

Question #104

Create a new ice cream topping that nobody's ever tried.

Question #105

What's one thing about your body you're thankful for?

THANKFUL
THANKFUL
THANKFUL

Question #106

If animals had jobs, what would a raccoon do?

Question #107

What do you think school lunches were like 100 years ago?

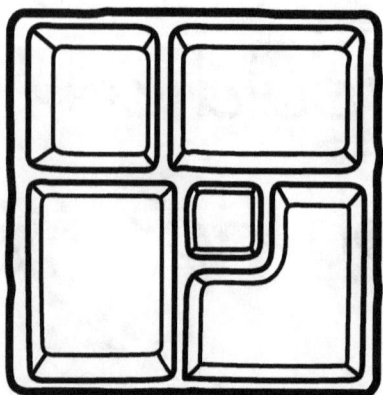

Question #108

What food
would you
make
disappear
forever?

Question #109

If you could be the best in the world at something, what would it be?

THE BEST

Question #110

If you could add one rule to holiday gift-giving, what would it be?

Question #111

Books

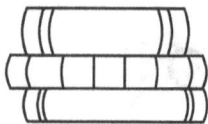

or

Movies?

Question #112

Who did you sit with at lunch or during a break?

Question #113

Would you rather play in leaves or decorate pumpkins?

Question #114

Why do people believe different things?

Question #115

What would you name your house if it had a name?

Question #116

If you could live in any fairy tale, which one would it be?

Question #117

If you had to be a bug for one day, which would you choose?

Question #118

When was the last time you surprised yourself?

Question #119

If your pet could suddenly talk, what would be the first thing it says?

Question #120

What kind of job can you do in pajamas?

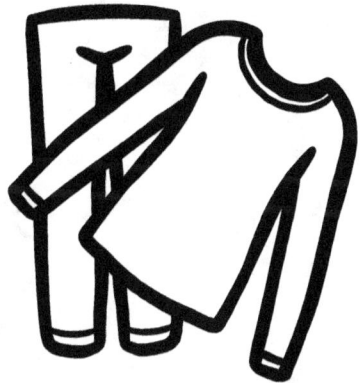

Question #121

What if your city made farting in public a musical performance?

Question #122

What's the best way to cool down on a hot day?

Question #123

Who is someone you've learned something important from?

Question #124

Would you rather have a robot best friend or a magical animal?

Question #125

What's something you're thankful for about the people at this table?

Interview

Sharpen your conversational toolkit and transform every meal into a masterclass in curiosity! Interviewing isn't just for job seekers-it's the art of asking the right questions, actively listening, and following up with genuine interest.

Ready to put your new interviewing skills to work? Start by posing these playful probing questions between bites, and feel free to invent your own:

What's the weirdest food combination you secretly love?

Which condiment best represents your personality—and how would you season your life?

If you could dine with any fictional character, who would it be and what's the first question you'd ask them?

What's one question you wish more people asked you at dinner?

If you had to summarize your life so far using only three ingredients, which would you choose?

Blankety-Blank Tales!

Provide your answer for each prompt by number. When you're done, flip to page 277 and fill in the corresponding blanks with your words. Then read the story—see if you can make it through without snorting!

1. Adjective:
2. Person's name:
3. Noun:
4. Silly food made-up name:
5. Another food:
6. Adjective:
7. Noun:
8. Noise:
9. Last name:
10. Verb ending in –ing:
11. Plural noun:
12. Verb ending in –ing:
13. Body part:
14. Person's name:
15. Food:
16. Number:
17. Exclamation:
18. Past-tense verb:
19. Adjective:

Question #126

What can you do if you see someone being unkind to someone else?

Question #127

If you could power up from eating your favorite food, what food would that be?

Question #128

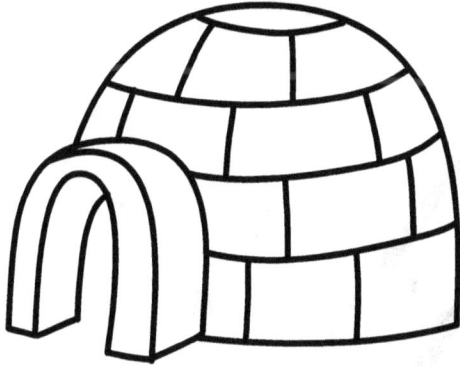

If you lived in an igloo, how would you decorate it?

Question #129

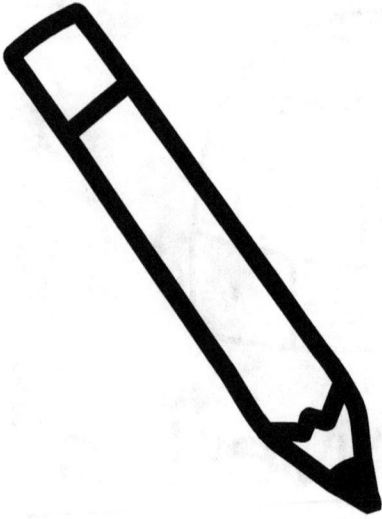

Design a pencil
that does
something special.

Question #130

What's one thing you're thankful you learned this week?

Beyond Grateful

Question #131

If a turtle challenged you to a race, would you accept?

Question #132

If you could change one thing in history, what would it be?

Question #133

If vegetables could talk, which one would be the sassiest?

Question #134

What's a place you dream of visiting one day?

Question #135

What would
your dream
gingerbread house
include?

Question #136

Super Speed

or

Super Strength?

Question #137

What's the silliest thing that's ever happened in your classroom?

Question #138

What's one goal you want to achieve this fall?

Question #139

Should people always follow the rules? Why or why not?

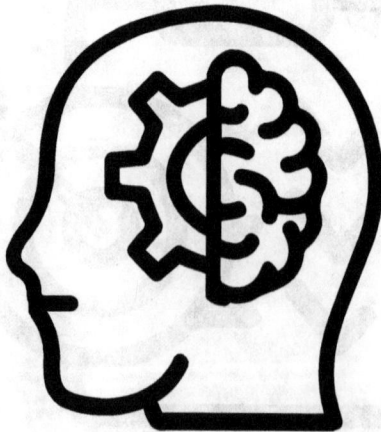

Question #140

What's the coolest thing about your kitchen?

Question #141

What would your royal crown look like?

Question #142

What's the first outdoor activity you want to do when it gets warm?

Question #143

What's something you've gotten better at this month?

Question #144

You wake up and everyone speaks in rhymes-how do you join in?

Question #145

What job would be perfect for a robot?

Question #146

What if no one was allowed to say the word "no"?

Question #147

If bugs had a summer camp, what would they do there?

Question #148

If you could swap lives with someone for a day, who would it be?

Question #149

Would you rather never need to sleep or never need to eat?

Question #150

What's your favorite way to help with dinner?

◆ Placemat Creation!

Unleash your imagination at the dinner table! On this page, you get to design the ultimate placemat-no rules, no limits. Will you fill it with flying pizza slices, a jungle of juicy fruits, or a galaxy of glowing pancakes? Grab your crayons, markers, or colored pencils and let your creativity run wild.

Word Search

Y	N	S	R	F	S	I	B	J	P	L	G	Z	Q	S
I	Z	P	E	E	O	A	Z	Z	I	P	O	M	U	E
M	P	A	G	V	L	C	Q	L	W	N	T	W	P	I
O	J	G	R	M	J	N	A	K	B	W	I	A	E	R
B	D	H	U	A	E	U	U	T	S	R	R	X	X	F
U	T	E	B	E	Z	G	Q	X	T	I	R	F	X	H
P	M	T	E	R	W	Q	O	M	E	L	U	H	H	C
F	V	T	S	C	M	B	C	H	A	L	B	K	H	N
I	O	I	E	E	G	R	O	D	K	U	M	N	M	E
Q	R	O	E	C	A	T	Y	A	Q	O	D	J	A	R
C	U	D	H	I	D	F	D	I	U	D	R	I	C	F
L	B	O	C	O	U	X	L	S	H	X	H	D	S	P
P	J	N	G	G	V	D	I	Q	D	S	N	R	B	S
G	Y	U	P	F	N	O	M	N	Q	N	U	L	Z	H
Y	B	T	L	I	U	D	A	L	A	S	H	S	X	O

CHEESEBURGER   HOTDOG
FRENCHFRIES   SUSHI
ICECREAM   SPAGHETTI
PIZZA   SALAD
TACO   DONUT
STEAK   BURRITO

Psssst...there isn't an answer key!
I believe in you!

Question #151

What color do you think kindness would be? Why?

Question #152

Would you rather have super hearing or super smell?

Question #153

What's your favorite winter-themed movie or book?

Question #154

Make up a silly alarm clock that gets you out of bed in the funniest way.

Question #155

What's a memory you're grateful for?

Beyond Grateful!

Question #156

What do you think chickens dream about?

Question #157

What do you think your great-great-grandkids will be like?

Question #158

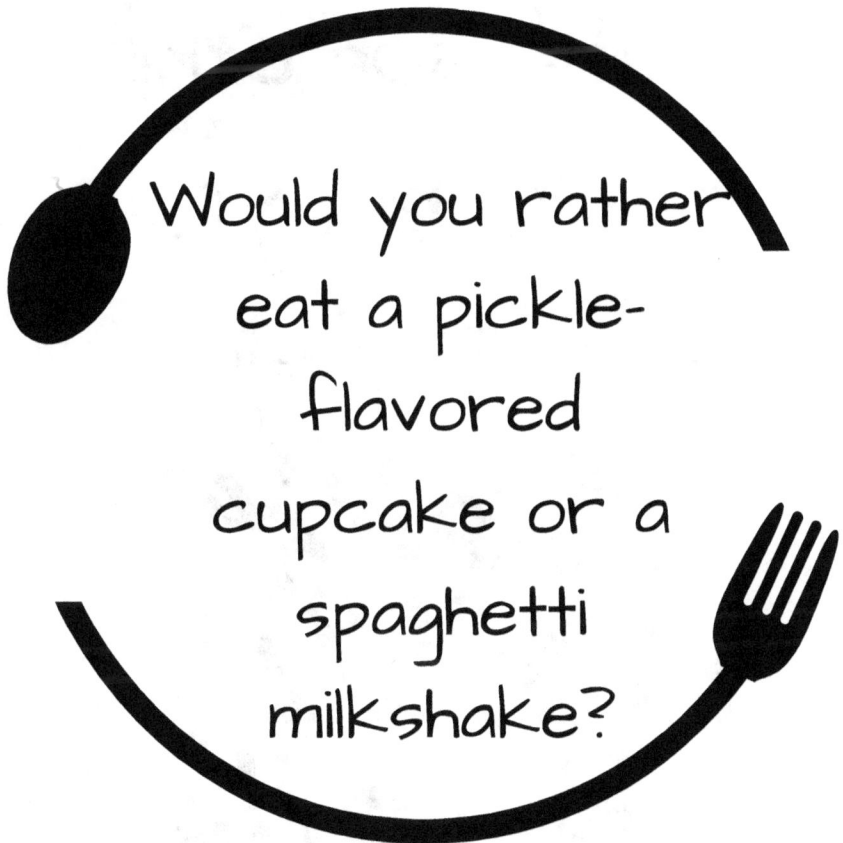

Would you rather eat a pickle-flavored cupcake or a spaghetti milkshake?

Question #159

What's something really big you want to learn?

Question #160

What's a silly holiday you'd like to celebrate with friends?

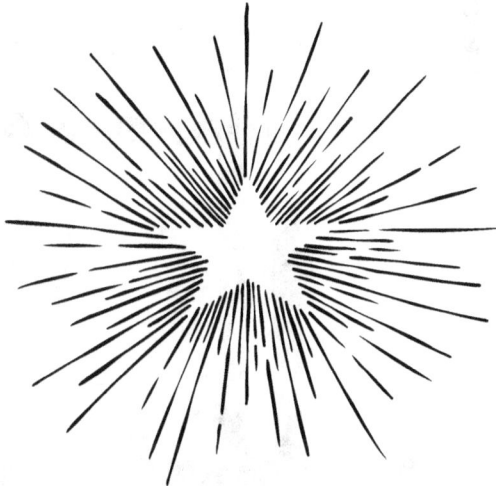

Question #161

Painting

Drawing?

Question #162

What's your favorite school snack or cafeteria meal?

Question #163

What's your favorite thing about night?

Question #164

Is it better to be really good at one thing or okay at many things?

Question #165

If you had a vending machine in the house, what would it give out?

Question #166

What magical object would you carry with you on an adventure?

Question #167

If you could design your own flower, what would it look like?

Question #168

When have you helped someone and felt awesome about it?

Question #169

You can shrink any object. What do you shrink and why?

Question #170

What kind of business would you start if you had $1,000?

Question #171

What if every meal had to start with a burp and end with a poem?

Question #172

What's the coolest summer outfit you've ever worn?

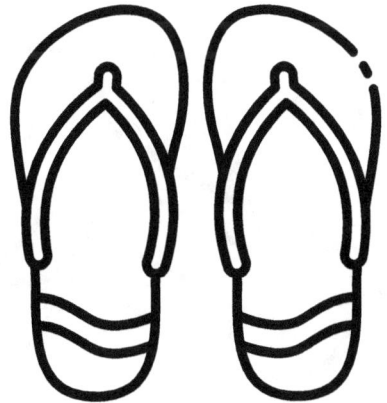

Question #173

What's one place you'd like to explore with a flashlight?

Question #174

Would you rather always have to hop or always have to sing when you talk?

Question #175

What's the most polite way to say you don't like something on your plate?

The Forbidden Page

You've reached the edge of a great mystery: the infamous Forbidden Page —page 405. Legend says that if you flip your eyes to that page, you'll unleash giggles so powerful they might shoot right out of your nose! I warned you: "Do not go there. Ever."

So, kiddo, I have to ask—did you sneak a peek when I told you not to? Be honest... your secret's safe with me (but the page might get you back)!

—Dr. Quirky Quickwit

☆Doodles ⚡

Question #176

How can you make someone laugh when they're sad?

Question #177

What would be your superhero catchphrase?

Question #178

What food
tastes best
when it's cold
outside?

Question #179

What kind of invention could help people who are always late?

Question #180

Who made your life better today-even just a little bit?

Question #181

What kind of music do you think elephants like?

Question #182

What futuristic gadget would you invent?

Question #183

If you could have a restaurant in your house, what would it serve?

Question #184

If you had your own museum, what would you fill it with?

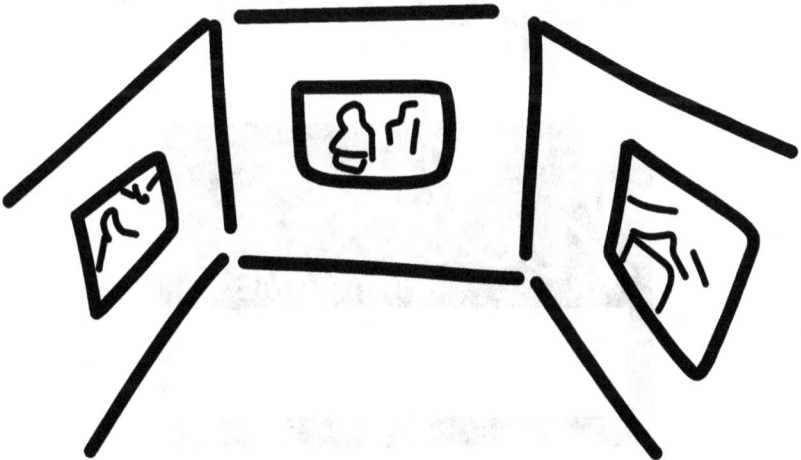

Question #185

What would your holiday nickname be (like "Captain Cozy" or "Princess Peppermint")?

hello
MY NAME IS

Question #186

SUMMER

OR

WINTER

Question #187

What's your favorite way to learn - reading, doing, or listening?

Question #188

What's your favorite fall family tradition?

FALL

Question #189

Can machines
ever feel
emotions?

Question #190

What's the best way to decorate the front door?

Question #191

If you opened a door to a fairy tale world, what's the first thing you'd see?

Question #192

What would your rain boots
look like if you designed them?

Question #193

What's a time you solved a problem on your own?

Question #194

You find a book that writes itself- what does it write about you?

Question #195

Would you rather work at an aquarium, a science lab, or a sports stadium?

JOB

Question #196

What if the rule was "no talking without a mustache"?

Question #197

What's your favorite thing to do with your friends during summer?

Question #198

If you could teleport anywhere after dinner tonight, where would you go?

Question #199

Would you rather always have cold hands or always have itchy socks?

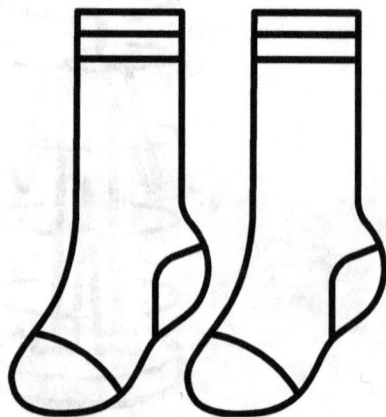

Question #200

What's the most creative dinner you can imagine using only foods that are yellow?

Jokes

LOL!

Knock, knock.
- Who's there?
- Lettuce.
- Lettuce who?
- Lettuce in, it's too chilly out here!

Knock, knock.
- Who's there?
- Kiwi.
- Kiwi who?
- Kiwi go out for dessert tonight?

Knock, knock.
- Who's there?
- Orange.
- Orange who?
- Orange you glad I brought orange slices?

JOKE

Knock, knock.
- Who's there?
- Taco.
- Taco who?
- Taco 'bout a great party —thanks for inviting me!

Knock, knock.
- Who's there?
- Butter.
- Butter who?
- Butter let me in before I melt!

HA HA HA HA HA

Knock, knock.
- Who's there?
- Olive.
- Olive who?
- Olive you and I miss you —open up!

Knock, knock.
- Who's there?
- Ice cream.
- Ice cream who?
- Ice cream every time I see a banana split!

3 Cheers for...

I'm grateful for...

I love when...

Question #201

What's a kind message you'd write on a billboard for the whole world to see?

Question #202

If you had
laser eyes,
what would
you use them
for?

Question #203

What's your ideal hot cocoa creation?

Question #204

Build a car that
runs on something
silly-like jellybeans
or giggles.

Question #205

What's your favorite thing in nature and why are you thankful for it?

Question #206

What would a squirrel do if it had your allowance?

Question #207

If you could only visit one decade from the past, which would it be?

MEMORY LANE

Question #208

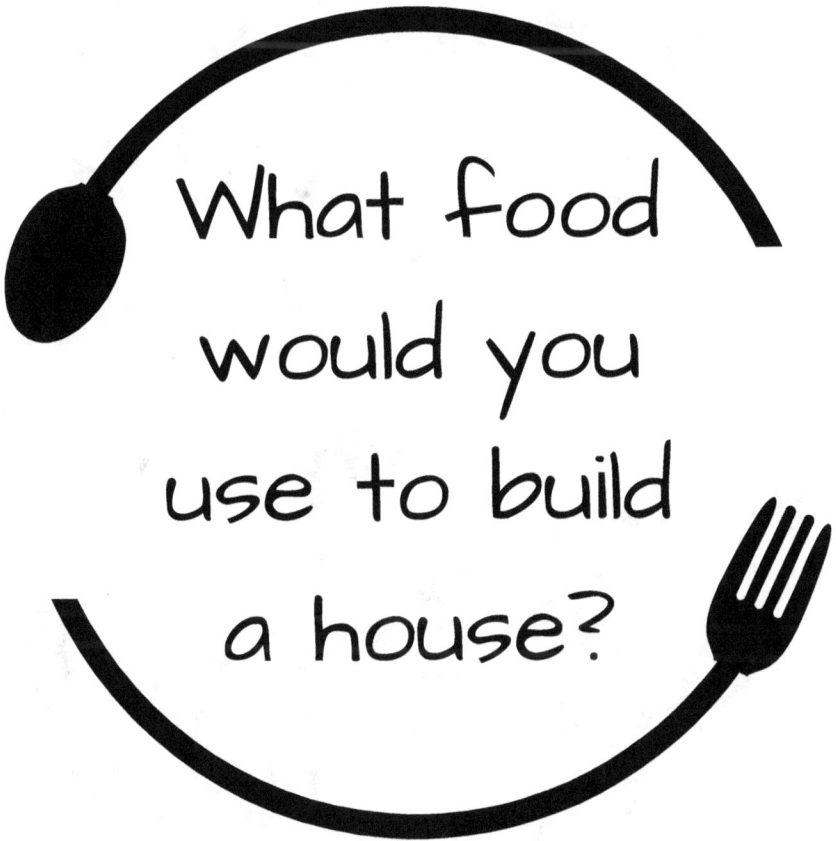

What food would you use to build a house?

Question #209

What does your dream day look like from start to finish?

AWESOME!

Question #210

What kind of holiday would animals celebrate?

Happy Holidays

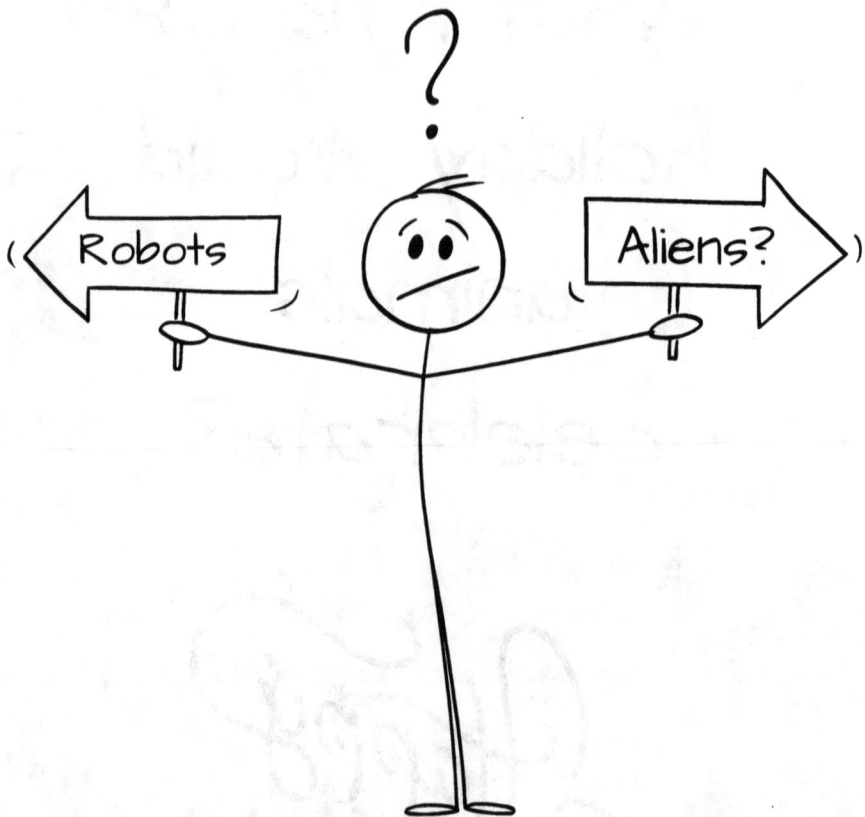

Question #212

If your school had a secret room, what would be inside it?

Question #213

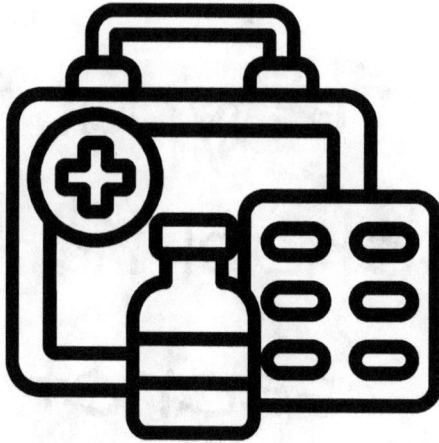

What would be
in your
survival kit?

Question #214

What's one idea you've had that you're really proud of?

Question #215

If every light switch controlled something silly, what would yours do?

Question #216

What's the name of the most mysterious fairy tale forest?

Question #217

Would you rather find a hidden treasure in your backyard or a rare flower in the woods?

☆Question #218

What's your best memory from this school year?

BEST

Question #219

If your dinner could magically talk, what would it say?

Question #220

What job do you think you'd be amazing at as a grown-up?

Question #221

What if "backwards day" happened once a week?

Question #222

What would you name a new kind of summer fruit?

Question #223

Who's someone you'd love to interview? What would you ask them?

Question #224

Would you rather live in a video game or in your favorite book?

Question #225

What would you name a cooking competition that takes place in your kitchen?

Menu

Design a menu for anything you can dream up—maybe an epic dragon's banquet with fire-roasted pizza and lava-licked cupcakes! Sketch out your appetizers, main course, and desserts, give each dish a zany name, and even draw little pictures beside them. Will your guests dine on Meteorite Meatballs or Pancake Parachutes?

Feelings Pie

Explore your emotions by coloring slices in four different pies-happiness, sadness, frustration, and calmness. First, think about how much of each feeling you've experienced today or this week, then color in the number of segments in each pie that matches your mood (for example, shade most of the Cherry Pie if you felt very happy, or just one or two slices of the Blueberry Pie if you felt a bit sad). Share your Feelings Pies with family or friends.

Happiness

Sadness

Frustration

Calmness

Question #226

How can you show kindness during a game or competition?

Question #227

What's a power that seems awesome but would actually be annoying?

Question #228

Would you rather ride a reindeer, a snowmobile, or a sled pulled by penguins?

Question #229

What would a vending machine that gives out surprises have in it?

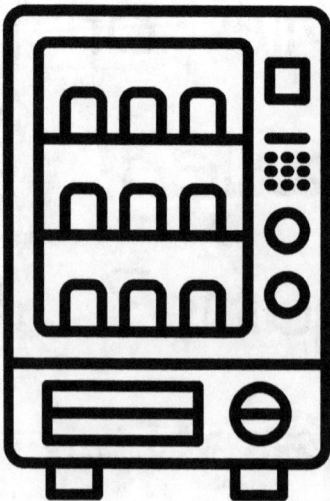

Question #230

What's a cozy place you're grateful for?

Question #231

What do you think
a sloth does on a
day off?

Question #232

If you had a time-traveling backpack, what would you keep in it?

Question #233

If pizza
could talk,
what would
it say?

Question #234

What's a talent you'd love to master?

Question #235

If you could decorate your house with anything (real or imaginary), what would you use?

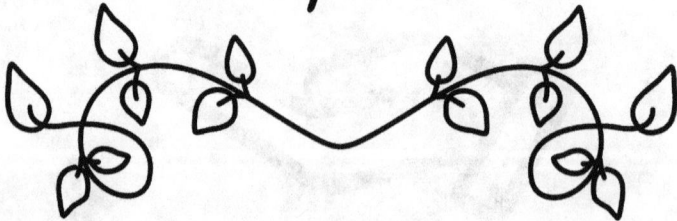

Question #236

Chocolate

OR

Vanilla?

Question #237

What's a
book
you loved
reading
in school?

Question #238

What's a new thing you'd like to learn this season?

Question #239

If you could solve one world problem, what would it be?

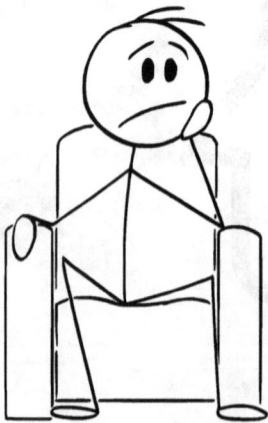

Question #240

What's a memory that happened in your living room?

Question #241

Would you rather ride a dragon or a unicorn?

Question #242

What sound makes you think of springtime?

Question #243

When did you feel really strong-mentally or physically?

Question #244

You find a genie but he only grants weird wishes-what do you wish for?

Question #245

What would it be like to work with your favorite celebrity?

Question #246

What if instead of birthdays, everyone celebrated "opposite day"?

Question #247

What's one thing you always forget to pack for a trip?

Question #248

What's the loudest place you've ever been?

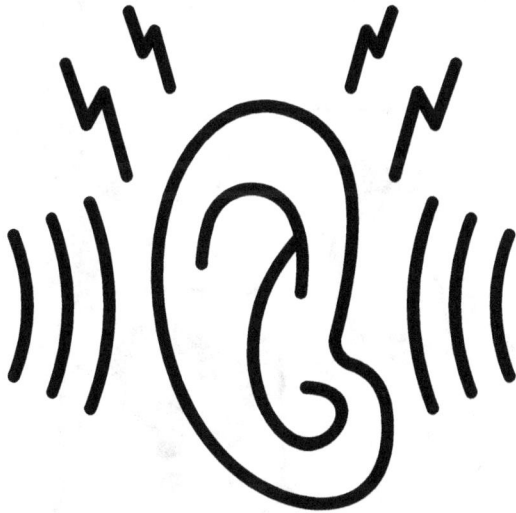

Question #249

Would you rather jump like a kangaroo or climb like a squirrel?

Question #250

If you had to sum up dinnertime in three words, what would they be?

1

2

3

To conquer the troll's riddles, hearken closely to each poetic clue, ponder its meaning, match it to a food, and boldly proclaim thy answer.

Encased in a brittle shell, I guard a yolk of gold—break my barrier if you're bold.

Golden and crisp, I lie in wait for ketchup's kiss; by handfuls I vanish— what starchy snack is this?

I enclose savory treasures in a pillowy sack, then plunge into boiling fate before I reach your fork.

Fizzy and bright in can or glass, I tickle your tongue with every gasp— what bubbly brew am I?

Twirl me 'round your fork in a river of red; long and slippery, I'm the ruler of the spread—who am I?

Blankety-Blank Tales: The Great School Lunch Adventure

One day at school, I sat down at the lunch table feeling [1]_____. My friend_____ plopped a [3]_____ onto my tray and said, "I dare you to try the [4]_____ !" As I took a bite, it tasted like [5]_____ mixed with [6]_____ [7]_____.

Suddenly, the lunchroom erupted in [8]_____, and the lunch monitor, Mr. [9]_____, started [10]_____ down the aisle with a tray full of [11]_____. I tried to escape by [12]_____, but my [13]_____ got stuck in my chair!

Just then, Principal [14]_____ announced over the loudspeaker, "Attention students: today's special dessert is [15]_____, so please line up in [16]_____ groups!" Everyone shouted "[17]_____!" and we formed a giant conga line to the cafeteria doors.

By the end of lunch, I felt [18]_____, but I couldn't wait to tell everyone about my [19]_____ adventure.

Question #251

How can you
be kind
to the
planet?

Question #252

What's the first rule in your superhero rulebook?

Question #253

What kind of soup makes you feel the coziest?

Question #254

Invent a silly but useful robot for the dinner table.

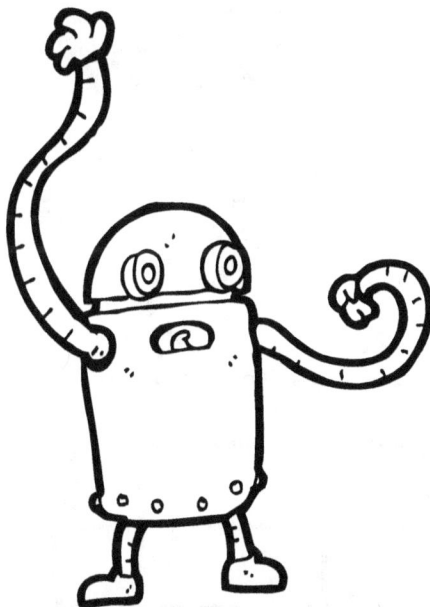

Question #255

What's one thing about school you're grateful for?

Question #256

If you had a tail, what kind would you want and why?

Question #257

What would happen if a pirate traveled to today?

Question #258

What fruit or veggie do you wish tasted like candy?

Question #259

If you could help the whole world in one way, what would you do?

Question #260

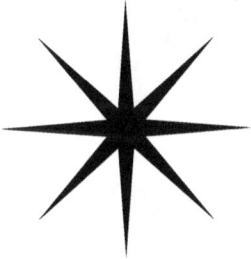

What would be the best way to spread holiday cheer?

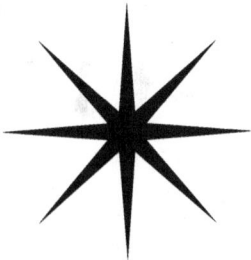

Question #261

Pool

or

Beach?

Question #262

Who's someone in your school that deserves a gold star?

Question #263

If you could carve any design into a pumpkin, what would it be?

Question #264

Do you think time is real or something humans made up?

TiME

Question #265

What's one thing in the house that always makes you laugh?

Question #266

If you were trapped in a tower, how would you escape?

Question #267

What's your favorite spring memory?

Spring Time

Question #268

What's a time you made someone else proud?

Question #269

You can fly-but only in silly ways. How would you fly?

Question #270

If you had a job at a museum, what would your title be?

Question #271

What if your house banned doors and replaced them with spaghetti curtains?

Question #272

What would be the best theme for a summer party?

Question #273

What makes a place feel like home to you?

Question #274

Would you rather only be able to whisper or only be able to shout?

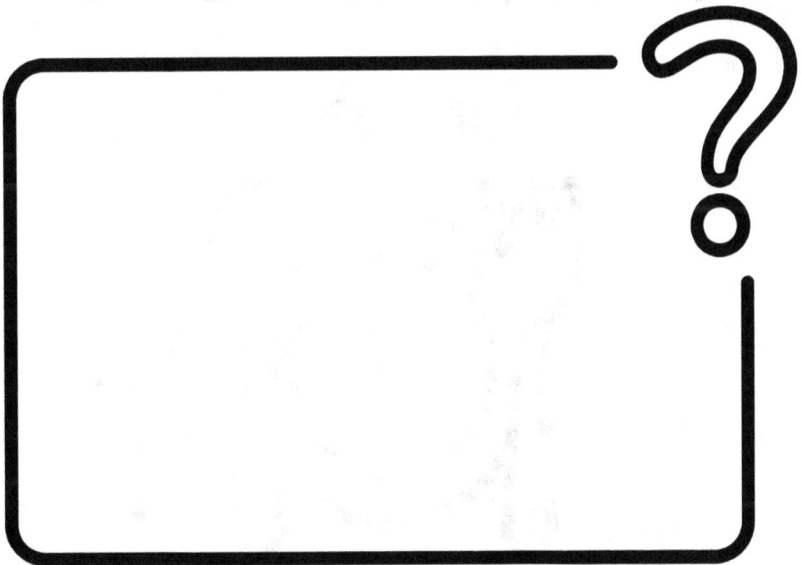

?

Question #275

What's something you'd like to ask someone else at this table about dinner?

Think of a family tradition you love—maybe it's baking cookies together at the holidays or backyard movie nights under the stars. If you don't have a tradition yet, dream up one you'd love—how about a family art party where everyone paints or a Sunday pancake picnic? Sketch the scene and add the people you'd share it with.

Meet Dr. Quirky Quickwit, the dinnertime scientist with wild curls, sparkly glasses, and a pocket full of curious questions ready to turn every meal into a fun experiment. When she's not coaxing jokes out of dancing veggies, she's busy juggling spaghetti strands, hosting spoon-flip contests, and inventing outrageous cupcake flavors (think pickle-pepper swirl!).

Question #276

Can you think
of a kind
thing to say
to yourself?

Question #277

Would you want to read minds? Why or why not?

Question #278

If you had a hot chocolate machine that made any flavor, what would you make?

Question #279

Create a TV remote that controls something unexpected.

Question #280

What's something your family does that makes you feel thankful?

Question #281

What animal would you want to switch places with for a day?

Question #282

What would the playground of the future look like?

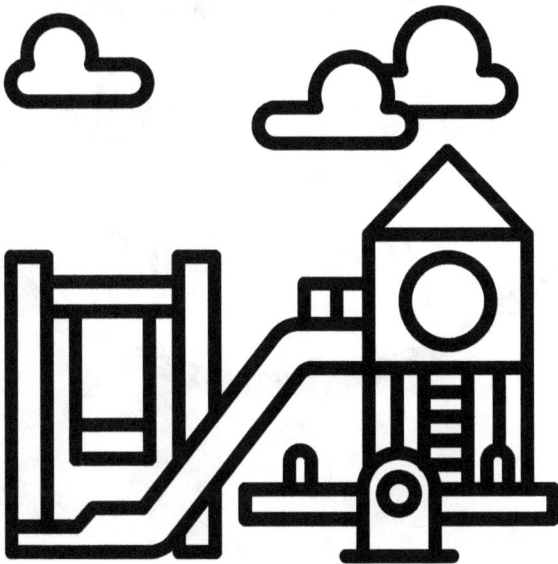

Question #283

If you
opened a
food truck,
what would
you sell?

Question #284

What kind of leader would you be if you were in charge?

Question #285

What's one tradition you'd like to start?

Question #286

Morning

A

B

Night?

Question #287

What's your favorite day of the school week and why?

Question #288

What's your favorite fall outdoor activity?

Question #289

What's something you're curious about right now?

Question #290

If the
TV only
played one
thing forever,
what should
it be?

Question #291

If you could invite three fairy tale characters to dinner, who would they be?

Question #292

If you were a bird building a nest, where would you put it?

Question #293

What's a game or sport you've gotten better at?

Question #294

You write a story and it comes true -what happens first?

Question #295

What kind of job could you do in total silence?

Question #296

What if all homework had to be written in Ketchup?

Question #297

What's your favorite game to play outside?

Question #298

What's one place you wish you could visit in every season?

Question #299

Would you rather live on a cloud or under the sea?

Question #300

What's something you think you think everyone at this table should try cooking?

The Forbidden Page

Deep in the heart of this book lies the infamous Forbidden Page —page 405—where only the bravest (or naughtiest) dare to peek. Legend whispers that it's filled with the silliest, most topsy-turvy questions you could ever imagine, but beware: once you glimpse its secrets, there's no turning back!

BINGO

As conversation flows, listen for any of the Bingo words/actions—when someone says one or does one...simply cross it off your card. See how fast your family completes a row, column, or diagonal. Yell "That's one good BINGO!" every time you get one! Keep the chatter going and see who can score the most Bingos by the end of the meal!

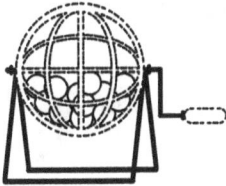

B	I	N	G	O
Friend	Joke	Excited	Yum!	Fruit
Game	Pet	Music	Work	Question
School	Laugh	Free Space	Grateful	Favorite
Sports	Today	Menu	Story	Dream
Surprise	Recipe	Vegetable	Celebrate	Weekend

Question #301

What's something kind you could do in secret?

Question #302

If you had x-ray vision, what would you use it for?

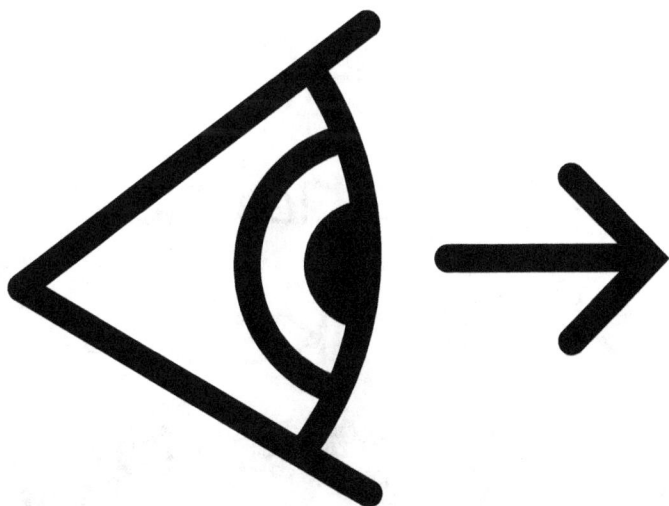

Question #303

If snowflakes were alive, what would their personalities be like?

Question #304

Invent a toy that never gets boring -what makes it fun?

Question #305

What's a fun moment you're glad happened recently?

FUN

Question #306

What sport would monkeys be best at?

Question #307

What would your future robot assistant be named?

Question #308

What's a funny name for a sandwich you invented?

Question #309

What does your
dream bedroom
look like?

Question #310

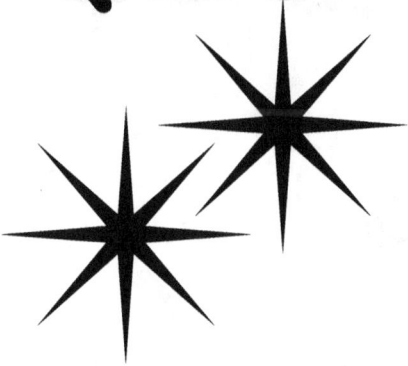

What do you think elves do in the off-season?

Question #311

 Cookies

or

Cake?

Question #312

What kind of school club would you want to start?

Question #313

Would you rather spend a chilly evening with hot cocoa or cider?

Question #314

Should everyone get the same things in life?

Question #315

What's a way to turn to turn cleaning into a competition?

Question #316

What's the funniest thing a troll might say under a bridge?

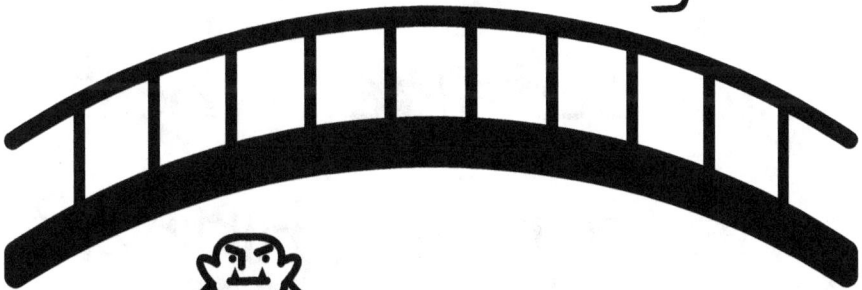

Question #317

What's your favorite thing to do outside when the sun is shining?

Question #318

What's your best dance move?

Question #319

A unicorn shows up at the dinner table. What do you feed it?

Question #320

What kind of job needs the most teamwork?

Question #321

What if no one could sit down unless they said a joke first?

Question #322

Would you rather roast marshmallows or make s'mores?

Question #323

What's a place you love visiting over and over again?

Question #324

Would you rather never have to brush your teeth or never have to clean your room?

Question #325

If you had a different theme night for every dinner, what should one be?

What do you think they have in their backpacks?

Poets Unite!

Gather your favorite meal memories and let your words sizzle on the page! Whether you're crafting a crunchy haiku, a savory sonnet, or a playful limerick, dinner poetry turns every bite into a verse. Experiment with rhythm like the clink of dishes, sprinkle in flavors like spices, and serve your poem with a garnish of fun!

Here is my French Fry Haiku:
Golden sticks of joy
Salt and laughter on my tongue
Crisp dreams in each bite

Question #326

If you had a "kindness jar," what would go inside it?

Question #327

If you could power up one person at this table, who would it be and what power would they get?

POWER

Question #328

What's the coziest place in your house during winter?

Question #329

Create a trampoline with a twist-what can it do?

Question #330

What's a chore you're glad you don't have to do?

Question #331

What would your pet say if it could give you advice?

Question #332

What slang do you think kids will use in the future?

Bussin'

Drip

Cap

Bet

g.o.a.t.

Sheesh

Salty

Sus

Stan

Hits different

Extra

Main character

Slaps

Question #333

What toppings would go on your ultimate waffle?

Question #334

What's one thing you hope people remember you for?

REMEMBER! →

Question #335

If you had a holiday sleigh, what would it look like?

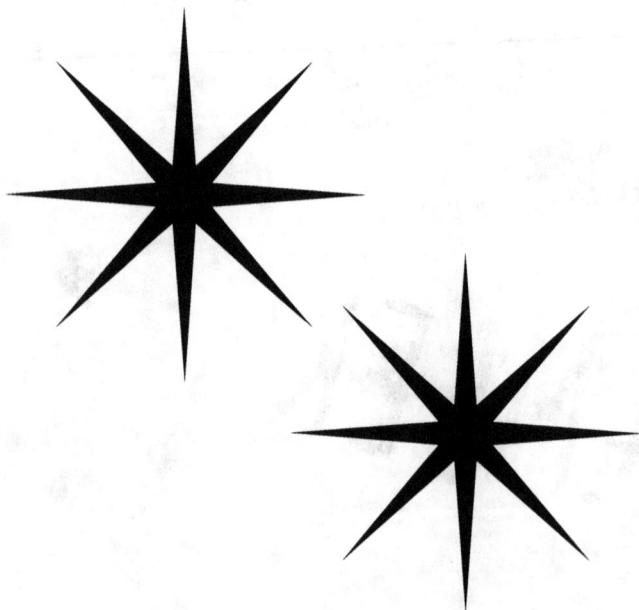

Question #336

Singing

OR

Dancing?

Question #337

What's your most organized school subject or folder?

Question #338

What would you name a leaf-collecting robot?

Question #339

Can you be happy and sad at the same time?

Question #340

What's your favorite favorite way to relax at home?

Question #341

What magical transportation would you use- flying carpet, dragon, or magic bubble?

Question #342

What would you name a pet bunny, duckling, or lamb?

Question #343

When did you feel
your most
focused?

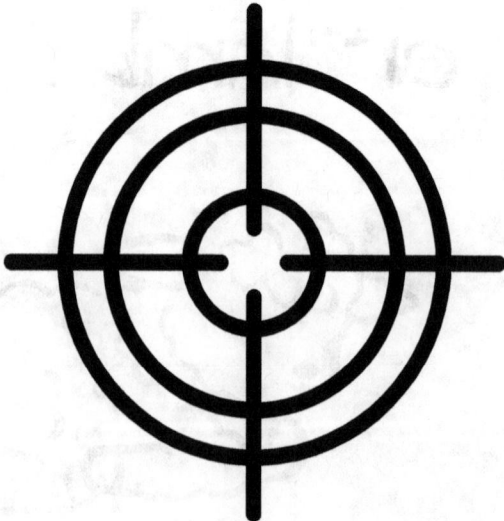

Question #344

If clouds were made of food, what would they taste like?

Question #345

What's a job that sounds boring but is actually cool?

Question #346

What if you could only walk backward on weekends?

Question #347

If you were the lifeguard of a mermaid pool, what would your rules be?

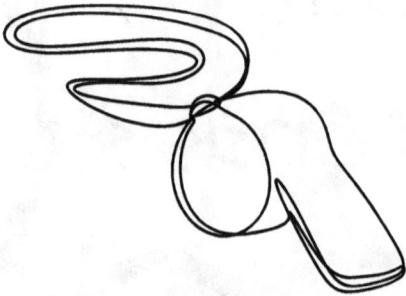

Question #348

What's the most peaceful place you can imagine?

Question #349

Would you rather turn everything you touch into gold or into slime?

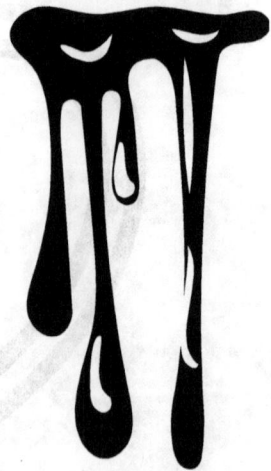

Question #350

Who would you trust most at this table to cook a surprise meal?

OMG!

doWr bacreSlrm

YAMLFI	TWES
AELPT	EALM
KFOR	ONSOP
RENDIN	IRFDEN
EADBR	EEHSEC

Draw the grossest Dinner EVER!

Question #351

If you could freeze time for one hour, what would you do?

Question #352

Pizza

or

Tacos?

Question #353

What would you do if you were in charge of the world for one week?

Question #354

Would you rather have cool powers with a silly name, or a cool name with silly powers?

YOUR PICK

Question #355

What if laughing was only allowed between 3 and 4 p.m.?

Question #356

If you could build something amazing, what would it be?

Question #357

If your shoes could walk around on their own, what would they do at home?

Question #358

Who would you want as your next-door neighbor in a dream world?

Question #359

You get to invent your own holiday- what is it called and how do you celebrate?

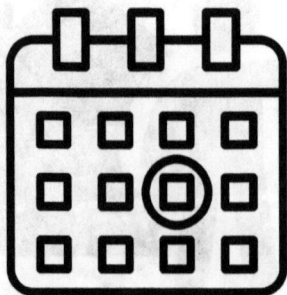

Holiday

Question #360

If you could be a detective, what kind of mysteries would you solve?

Question #361

What's the best use for a big cozy blanket?

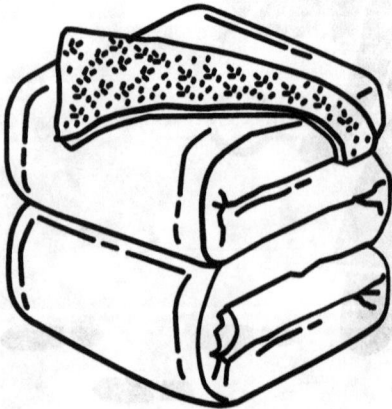

Question #362

If your spoon
could do
something magical,
what would you
invent it to do?

Question #363

What animal would you send as an ambassador to aliens?

Question #364

What if there was a rule that you had to high-five everyone you saw-even squirrels?

Question #365

What's the best joke you've ever told?

Dear Mom,

Guess what? I've officially embarked on the epic quest of writing a 400-page book—a colossal tome of towering tomfoolery and profound pondering, all wrapped up in one delicious dinner-time package. Picture this: young adventurers tackling the silliest and most soul-stirring questions ever devised, from "If a spaghetti noodle could talk, what would it whisper?" to "Which constellation best describes your broccoli dreams?"—all while cheerfully chewing on chowder, munching on macaroni, snarfing spaghetti, and grazing on gumbo. It's the ultimate banquet of brain-teasers and belly-fillers!

None of this whirlwind of whisking words into wonderland would have been possible without your unwavering encouragement (and your uncanny ability to turn every meal into a moment of magic). Thank you for inspiring me to sprinkle a little zest and zaniness into every dinner and for teaching me that the best conversations happen over shared slices of pie—or pork chops, pizza, or peanuts in a pinch!

With heaps of hearty hugs and ladles of laughter,

Dr. Quirky Quickwit

Congrats

You did it!

You've journeyed through every question, shared your funniest stories, and filled these pages with your imagination. You're officially a Dinner Table Question Champion! Now go ahead and celebrate: give yourself a high-five, throw a little victory dance, and know that your creativity made every meal a magical adventure. Great job-and keep dreaming up more questions to explore!

📅 Leap Year

You may have asked yourself, "The book only has 365 questions, but what if I'm reading this during a Leap Year? I'm missing a question! Whatever shall I do?"

Well, you're in luck!

I've included an extra question for that very instance!

Fun Fact: Why do we have Leap Year? Well, Earth actually needs about 365¼ days to circle the Sun, not exactly 365. That extra quarter-day adds up, so every four years we dump in an extra day—February 29—to keep our calendar lined up with the seasons. Without it, soon summer would sneak into winter, and spring would show up in autumn!

Question #366

Would you rather have spaghetti hair or popcorn feet?

BONUS

BONUS

BONUS

Forbidden Page

Oh no! You peeked! Because you looked at this forbidden page, all the words that were here have vanished into thin air! Quick, close the book before the rest of the words escape!

h

o

w

S

R

j

g

e

t

d

c

a

Question
Authority

This certificate is presented to

_____

Your relentless curiosity and enthusiasm have powered this adventure from start to finish—and your support has made our journey a smashing success!

Dr. Quirky Quickwit

DR. QUIRKY QUICKWIT

The President

THE PREZ

Got a dazzling question, a side-splitting joke, or a charming family yarn? Dr. Quirky Quickwit is all ears! As the mastermind behind these totally radical questions and the self-proclaimed "Scientist of Dinnertime," she's on a perpetual quest for new conversation starters to enliven your table talk.

Zap your questions, jokes, or tales to AskDrQuirky@gmail.com, and you might just find them in a future issue of Curious Quest!

Your Questions

Got a mystery on your mind or a silly thought you can't shake? Draw a doodle of your question, spell it out in neat letters-or go wild with colors and shapes. Fill up these pages with every "huh?" and "what if?" that pops into your head-there are no wrong questions here!

The End.

For now...

Probably?

www.ingramcontent.com/pod-product-compliance
Lightning Source LLC
Chambersburg PA
CBHW052119270326
41930CB00012B/2678